DO YOU BELIEVE?
ALIENS

by Natalie Deniston

pogo

Ideas for Parents and Teachers

Pogo Books let children practice reading informational text while introducing them to nonfiction features such as headings, labels, sidebars, maps, and diagrams, as well as a table of contents, glossary, and index.

Carefully leveled text with a strong photo match offers early fluent readers the support they need to succeed.

Before Reading

- "Walk" through the book and point out the various nonfiction features. Ask the student what purpose each feature serves.
- Look at the glossary together. Read and discuss the words.

Read the Book

- Have the child read the book independently.
- Invite him or her to list questions that arise from reading.

After Reading

- Discuss the child's questions. Talk about how he or she might find answers to those questions.
- Prompt the child to think more. Ask: Do you believe aliens exist? Why or why not?

Pogo Books are published by Jump!
5357 Penn Avenue South
Minneapolis, MN 55419
www.jumplibrary.com

Copyright © 2025 Jump!
International copyright reserved in all countries. No part of this book may be reproduced in any form without written permission from the publisher.

Library of Congress Cataloging-in-Publication Data

Names: Deniston, Natalie, author.
Title: Aliens / by Natalie Deniston.
Description: Minneapolis, MN: Jump!, Inc., [2025]
Series: Do you believe? | Includes index.
Audience: Ages 7-10
Identifiers: LCCN 2023054580 (print)
LCCN 2023054581 (ebook)
ISBN 9798892132152 (hardcover)
ISBN 9798892132169 (paperback)
ISBN 9798892132176 (ebook)
Subjects: LCSH: Extraterrestrial beings—Juvenile literature. | Unidentified flying objects—Sightings and encounters—Juvenile literature. | Conspiracy theories—Juvenile literature.
Classification: LCC BF2050 .D459 2025 (print)
LCC BF2050 (ebook)
DDC 001.942–dc23/eng/20231201
LC record available at https://lccn.loc.gov/2023054580
LC ebook record available at https://lccn.loc.gov/2023054581

Editor: Jenna Gleisner
Designer: Emma Almgren-Bersie

Photo Credits: IG Digital Arts/Shutterstock, cover (alien); JLStock/Shutterstock, cover (corn); BrilliantEye/iStock, cover (moon); ktsdesign/Shutterstock, 1 (UFO), 23; xijian/iStock, 1 (car); Design Projects/Shutterstock, 3; adventtr/iStock, 4; Marti Bug Catcher/Shutterstock, 5; Islam Moawad/iStock, 6-7; Chronicle/Alamy, 8; Courtesy, Fort Worth Star-Telegram Photograph Collection, Special Collections, The University of Texas at Arlington Library, Arlington, Texas, 9; Sky_Blue/iStock, 10-11; World History Archive/Alamy, 12; REDPIXEL.PL/Shutterstock, 12-13; yuelan/iStock, 14-15; Trinity Mirror/Mirrorpix/Alamy, 16-17; joshimerbin/Shutterstock, 18; NASA/JPL-Caltech, 19; m-gucci/iStock, 20-21.

Printed in the United States of America at Corporate Graphics in North Mankato, Minnesota.

TABLE OF CONTENTS

CHAPTER 1
Life Out There? 4

CHAPTER 2
Mysterious Sightings 8

CHAPTER 3
Talking to Aliens 18

QUICK FACTS & TOOLS
Timeline 22
Glossary 23
Index 24
To Learn More 24

CHAPTER 1
LIFE OUT THERE?

There are countless **planets** in our **universe**. Earth is the only one with known life. People, plants, and animals live here. Could other planets have life, too?

Some people believe in aliens. These are creatures from other planets. Some think they have been to Earth!

CHAPTER 1

Some people think aliens do mysterious things. Like what? The Egyptian pyramids are made of stone. Each block weighs about 2.5 tons (2.3 metric tons). Could **ancient** Egyptians have moved them? Some people don't think so. They believe aliens did it. If aliens built pyramids, what else could they do?

CHAPTER 1

CHAPTER 2

MYSTERIOUS SIGHTINGS

In July 1947, a man went to the sheriff's office in Roswell, New Mexico. He said a flying disk crashed on his farm. He found pieces. The U.S. Army went to **investigate**. Soon, news of a **flying saucer** spread across the country.

piece from crash

The Army said it was a **weather balloon**. But many people did not believe that. They thought it was an alien spaceship.

weather balloon

CHAPTER 2

More people across America saw UFOs. UFO is short for "**unidentified** flying object." A UFO can be any unknown object in the sky. Many are fast. They have strange lights. Some make sounds. Others are silent.

Some UFOs can be explained. Like what? They might just be airplanes. Others are not explained. Could they be alien spaceships?

WHAT DO YOU THINK?

Some people claim to see USOs. These are unidentified **submerged** objects. What do you think these could be?

CHAPTER 2

In 1961, Betty and Barney Hill were driving late at night. They saw a strange light in the sky. They followed it. Suddenly, it was morning! The light was gone. They couldn't remember the rest of the night.

Later, they said they remembered. They believed they were **abducted** by aliens. They said aliens studied them. Then the aliens brought the Hills back to their car.

Betty and Barney Hill

TAKE A LOOK!

What do Betty and Barney Hill say happened? Take a look!

SEPTEMBER 19, 1961

10:00 p.m.
The Hills start driving from Colebrook, New Hampshire. They plan to get home to Portsmouth, New Hampshire, around 3:00 a.m.

10:30–11:00 p.m.
They see a strange light in the sky. At first, they think it is an airplane.

11:00 p.m.
The Hills follow the light. They watch it with binoculars. They see beings. Then Betty and Barney fall asleep.

SEPTEMBER 20, 1961

Unknown
The Hills wake up. They drive home.

5:00 a.m.
The Hills arrive home.

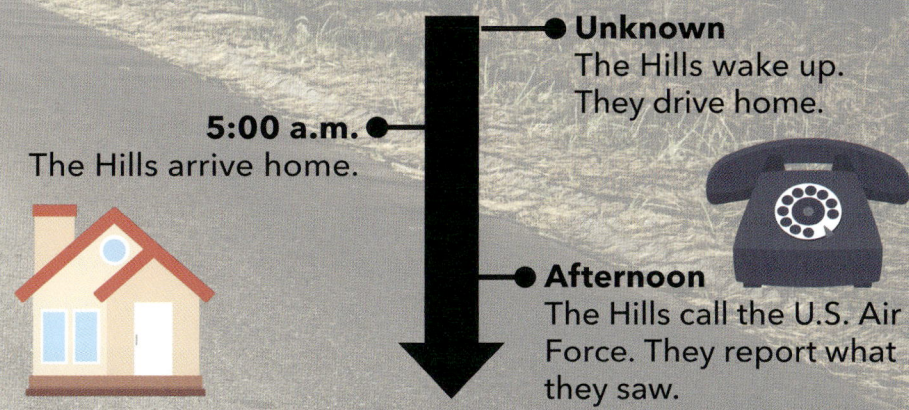

Afternoon
The Hills call the U.S. Air Force. They report what they saw.

CHAPTER 2 — 13

The year was 1976. A farmer in Wiltshire, England, was in his wheat field. He found something strange. The wheat was pressed down. It made a detailed pattern. But there were no footprints. There were no vehicle tracks. Who or what made the design?

WHAT DO YOU THINK?

One **theory** said an alien ship pressed the wheat down. Then it flew away. That is why there were no footprints. What do you think made the design?

CHAPTER 2

More patterns appeared. People called them **crop circles**. In 1991, Doug Bower and Dave Chorley came forward. They said they made more than 200 crop circles. They made the one in Wiltshire. How? They used a piece of wood to press the crops down.

But crop circles appeared in other countries, too. Some were in the United States. Where did they come from?

CHAPTER 2 17

CHAPTER 3
TALKING TO ALIENS

If you could talk to aliens, would you? What would you say? In 1977, **NASA** decided to try. It sent two spacecraft into outer space. They are still there.

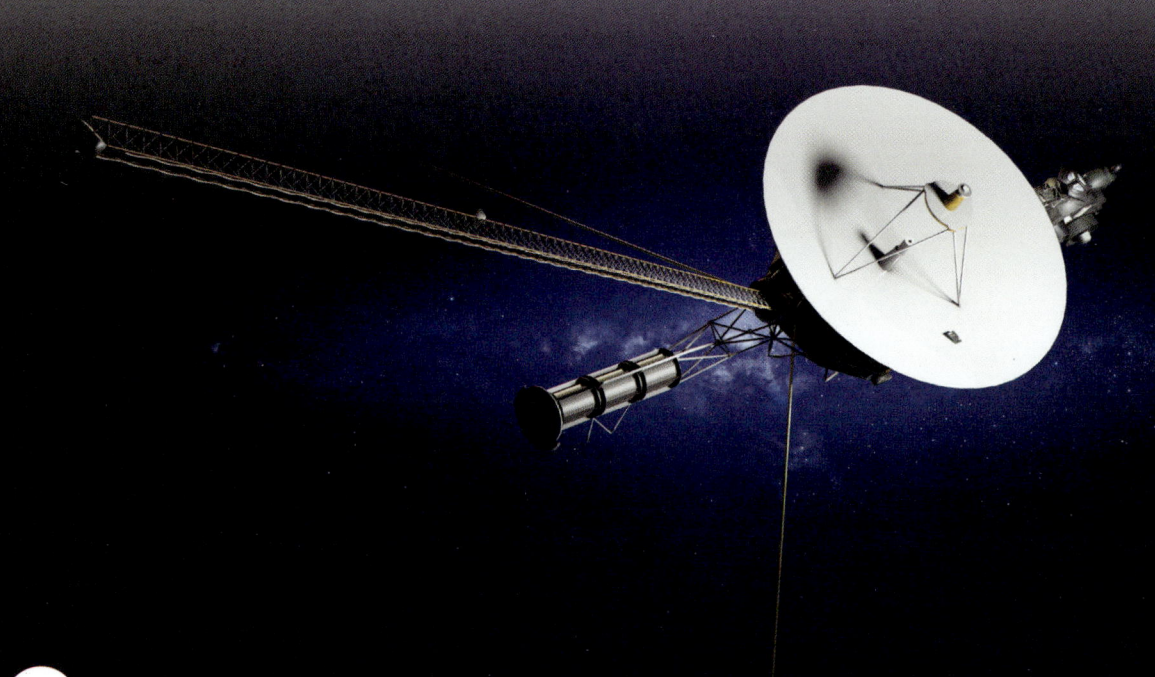

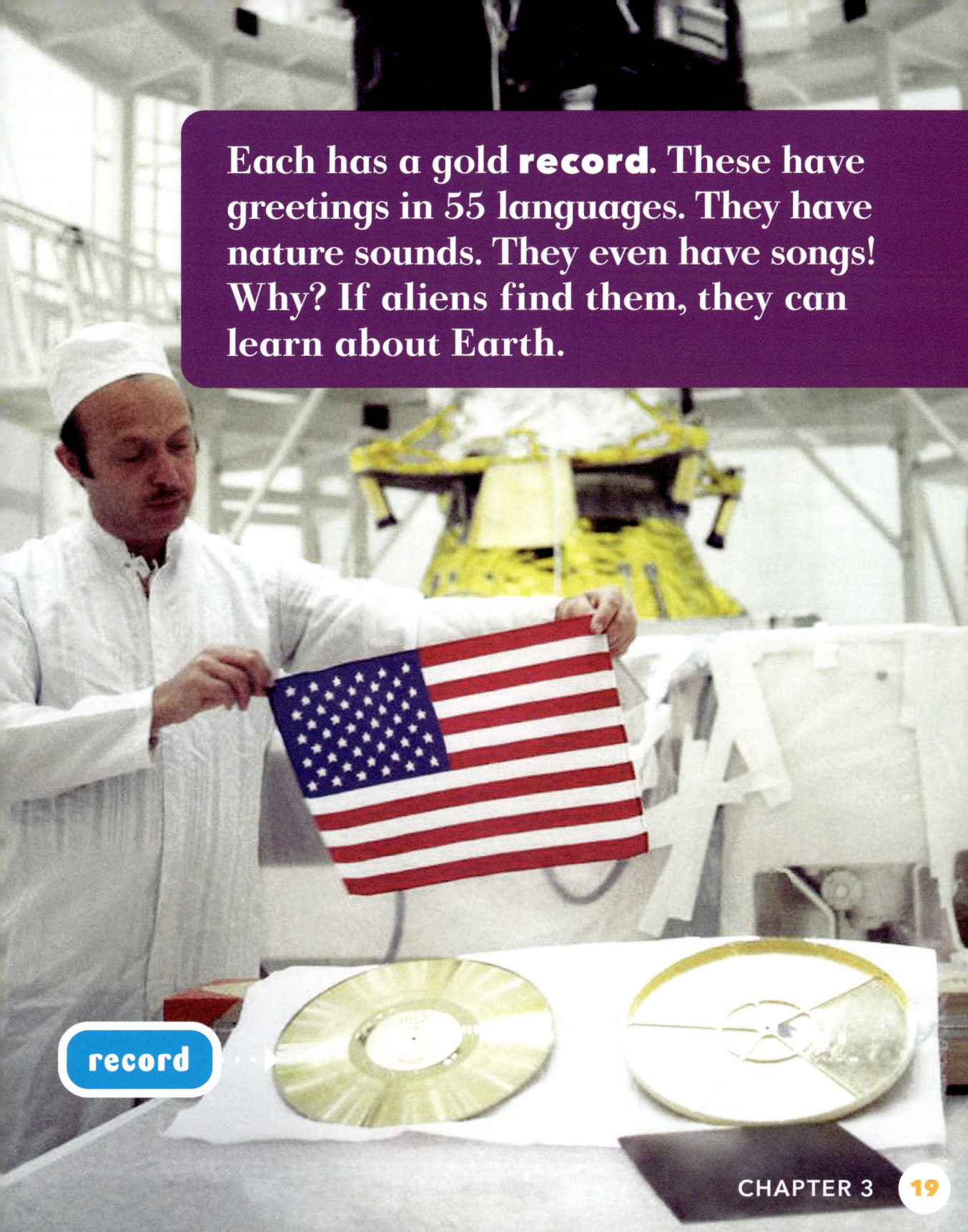

Each has a gold **record**. These have greetings in 55 languages. They have nature sounds. They even have songs! Why? If aliens find them, they can learn about Earth.

record

CHAPTER 3 • 19

In 2023, the U.S. government held a **hearing**. Members of the military talked about seeing UFOs. Some said the government had proof of aliens. Others disagreed.

Do you believe aliens are real? Do you think they have come to Earth?

DID YOU KNOW?

The U.S. Air Force looked into more than 12,000 UFO reports. When? Between 1947 and 1969. It was called Project Blue Book. It did not find proof of aliens.

QUICK FACTS & TOOLS

TIMELINE

Some people believe aliens have been visiting Earth for thousands of years. Take a look!

2550-2490 BCE
The Egyptian pyramids are built. Some people believe aliens made them.

JULY 7, 1947
An object crashes near Roswell, New Mexico. Some believe it is an alien spacecraft.

SEPTEMBER 19-20, 1961
Betty and Barney Hill claim to be abducted by aliens.

1976
Doug Bower and Dave Chorley begin making crop circles in and around Wiltshire, England.

AUGUST 20, 1977
Voyager 2 spacecraft launches. It has a gold record to tell aliens about Earth.

SEPTEMBER 5, 1977
Voyager 1 spacecraft launches. It also has a gold record.

SEPTEMBER 9, 1991
Doug Bower and Dave Chorley admit to making crop circles.

JULY 26, 2023
The U.S. government has a hearing about UFOs. People argue if there is proof of aliens.

GLOSSARY

abducted: Taken away by force.

ancient: Very old or from the very distant past.

crop circles: Large patterns created by flattening crops in a field.

flying saucer: A disk-shaped flying object said to be driven by aliens.

hearing: A special government meeting at which people gather information.

investigate: To gather information about something.

NASA: The National Aeronautics and Space Administration. NASA is the United States' space agency.

planets: Large bodies that orbit, or travel in circles around, the Sun.

record: A disk with grooves on which sound, especially music, is recorded.

submerged: Beneath the surface of a liquid, especially water.

theory: An idea or opinion that is based on some facts or evidence but is not proven.

unidentified: Not known or recognized.

universe: All existing matter and space.

weather balloon: A balloon that carries machines high into the air to measure weather or wind conditions.

INDEX

abducted 12
Bower, Doug 17
Chorley, Dave 17
crop circles 17
Earth 4, 5, 19, 21
Egyptian pyramids 6
flying saucer 8
Hill, Barney and Betty 12, 13
NASA 18
planets 4, 5
Project Blue Book 21
record 19
Roswell, New Mexico 8
spaceship 9, 11, 14
UFO 11, 21
universe 4
U.S. Air Force 13, 21
U.S. Army 8, 9
U.S. government 21
USOs 11
weather balloon 9
Wiltshire, England 14, 17

TO LEARN MORE

Finding more information is as easy as 1, 2, 3.

1. Go to www.factsurfer.com
2. Enter "aliens" into the search box.
3. Choose your book to see a list of websites.